BEAVERS
& OTHER RODENTS
A PORTRAIT OF THE ANIMAL WORLD

PAUL STERRY

TODTRI

This book was designed and produced by TODTRI Book Publishers
P.O. Box 572, New York, NY 10116-0572 FAX: (212) 695-6984

Printed and bound in Korea

ISBN 1-57717-077-6

Author: Paul Sterry

Publisher: Robert M. Tod
Editor: Edward Douglas
Assistant Editor: Elaine Luthy
Book Designer: Mark Weinberg
Typesetting: Command-O Design

PHOTO CREDITS
Photo Source/Page Number

Dembinsky Photo Associates
Mike Barlow 7
Dominique Braud 10, 14 (top), 24–25, 55, 66, 71
Sharon Cummings 16, 28, 36
John Gerlach 48
Darrell Gulin 3, 61
Ed Kanze 8–9
Skip Moody 4 (top), 56–57
Stan Osolinski 23
Rod Planck 4 (bottom)
Jim Roetzel 44
Carl R. Sams 20, 68–69

Jeff Foott 63 (top)

Brian Kenney 27–28, 45 (top), 50

Tom and Pat Leeson 6, 11 (bottom), 13, 14 (bottom), 15, 26 (left), 27 (top),
29, 30 (top), 32, 34, 35, 38 (top), 40–41, 52 (top), 53, 63 (bottom)

Joe McDonald 19, 31, 39, 51 (bottom), 64 (top & bottom), 65

Nature Photographers Ltd.
Paul Sterry 42 (top & bottom), 43, 60, 62, 70

Picture Perfect 54
Warren Jacobi 17 (top)
Robert Pollack 22 (top)
Hans Reinhard 5,
Wayne Shields 11 (top)

Tom Stack & Associates
John Cancalosi 37, 38 (bottom), 46 (top), 52 (bottom), 58, 59
Bill Everitt 45 (bottom)
Jeff Foott 30 (bottom)
Victoria Hurst 21
Thomas Kitchin 22 (bottom), 47
Joe McDonald 17 (bottom), 51 (top)
Wendy Shattil/Rob Rozinski 33, 46 (bottom)
John Shaw 49
Robert C. Simpson 18 (top)
Diana L. Stratton 12
Dave Watts 18 (bottom), 67

INTRODUCTION

After a winter spent in hibernation, this hoary marmot is foraging for food amid a sea of lupines in North America's Mount Rainier National Park. The animal must lay down large reserves of fat to sustain it through the following winter's slumber.

Rodents are among the most successful of all mammals, and, in their range and numbers, among those most closely linked to the spread and progress of man. Some of the seventeen hundred or so species that make up the group have followed in the wake of man, taking advantage of newly created habitats and feeding opportunities resulting from farming and urbanization, while others have declined as the human population has grown in size and influence. Some rodents help spread contagious diseases, but by contrast, a few species have become cherished pets. There is even one, the beaver, over which wars have been fought.

There is scarcely a terrestrial habitat where rodents of one species or another do not occur. Grasslands are the domain of mice and voles, while forests are home to squirrels and their relatives. Wetland habitats present few problems for these versatile mammals, with beavers, capybaras, and coypus adopting an almost aquatic lifestyle. Marmots living on mountaintops, gerbils inhabiting deserts, and lemmings proliferating on the arctic tundra—the list goes on and on. Only the open sea and the skies appear to be out of bounds to rodents, although flying squirrels make a valiant attempt at conquering the latter.

Although most rodents conform to a rather squat and superficially uniform body plan, the size range seen across the group as a whole is enormous. Some of the smallest mice may weigh just a few grams, while that giant among rodents, the capybara, is the size of a sheep and weighs more than 135 pounds (60 kilograms). The group's size range is also complemented by a varied diet, despite the fact that all rodents share the same basic gnawing method of feeding. Add to this a prodigious reproductive rate and a lifestyle that often involves social as well as sociable behavior, and it is little wonder that rodents have an impact on all our lives.

The diet of most rodents—mainly nuts, seeds, and cereals—may be rich in oils and proteins, but it is usually rather dry. Not surprisingly, therefore, many species, except those adapted to desert environments, pay regular visits to pools to drink.

This yawning black-tailed prairie dog clearly shows the incisor teeth typical of all rodents. The teeth's razor-sharp edge is achieved and maintained by their opposing action causing wear against one another.

Like all other rodents, hamsters gnaw their food using their incisor teeth. When large objects such as nuts are opened, the paws are generally used to manipulate the food into the orientation best suited to the action of the teeth.

BUILDERS AND DESTROYERS

Rodents as a group comprise a large proportion of living mammals. Apart from their similarities, there is a wide range of habits and behavior among these animals. Before considering the characteristics of rodents in general, it is useful to examine two well-known animals that have dramatically affected their surroundings and whose lifestyles are very different: the beaver and the rat.

Beavers

It is high summer in Alaska's Denali National Park, a season when that land is at last free of snow, and colorful flowers and a mosaic of pools and wetlands adorn the landscape. Picture a bank beside one of the myriad tranquil ponds, where the reflection of Mount McKinley and plants fringing the water margin are mirrored to perfection in the glasslike surface. Only an occasional gust of wind or a family of ducks—perhaps American widgeon—swimming peacefully mars the reflection. Suddenly, this peaceful scene is shattered by a loud splash, sending ripples far and wide across the water. Catching the whiff of a roving grizzly bear, a beaver has plunged to safety, the water providing a haven from all but the most persistent predators.

Bears may be the largest predators in Denali and elsewhere in the northern lands, but beavers are in many ways the true masters. This North American animal is perhaps the most industrious, modifying the world around it to increase its chances of survival. More than any other, with the possible exception of man, the beaver has shaped the arctic landscape—and by doing so, has benefited almost all the creatures that share this environment.

The North American beaver is the continent's largest rodent, with adults weighing up

Following page: Viewed from above, the beaver's amazingly broad and flattened tail can be appreciated, and its scaly texture clearly seen. This superbly evolved anatomical feature provides speedy propulsion and directional control during swimming.

During summer, the leaves and shoots of trees such as willows and aspens are extremely important in the beaver's diet. A supply of logs and branches is harvested in the autumn and stored in the beavers' moat. It is upon these reserves that the animals rely to see them through the frozen winter months.

When felling trees such as this aspen, beavers use techniques similar to those of human foresters. Given the animal's size, it is important that the tree should fall in a direction suitable for its subsequent removal.

On land the beaver may appear cumbersome, moving with a waddling, shuffling gait. In water, however, the animal is in its element and swims with ease and grace. As adaptations to this amphibious lifestyle, the ears and nostrils close when the beaver is submerged, and a special membrane protects the eyes.

to 65 pounds (30 kilograms), and is the second largest rodent in the world, after its water-loving cousin, the capybara. Even though it has been hunted for centuries and its numbers and range have contracted northwards, the North American beaver is still comparatively widespread and easy to see in the appropriate environments. Commercial hunting for pelts continues to this day, but thankfully, a more sustainable approach has been adopted, rather than the wholesale slaughter seen in centuries past. A second species, the European beaver, has been less fortunate than its New World cousin; both its range and its numbers have been drastically reduced due to hunting and habitat degradation.

Beavers live in family groups consisting of an adult male and female, which pair for life,

along with the young from the current year and occasionally offspring from the previous season as well. The social structure of the group is maintained through a hierarchy, relative dominance being decided according to age and maturity. Beavers mate in the winter and give birth to young, known as kits, in the spring. Unlike the young of rats and mice, baby beavers are born with their eyes open and with a coat of fur. Although active and capable of swimming soon after birth, their buoyancy prevents them from swimming down the submerged lodge exit during their first few weeks. Thereafter, they partake of family life to the full and generally remain with the family group for at least a year.

At the heart of any beaver community is the lodge, a large conical mound of mud, stones,

Regular inspection and repair of both the dam and the lodge are essential activities in the routine life of the beaver. Building materials such as logs and twigs are seldom deployed without being fashioned in some way by the animal to better suit the job at hand.

Beavers are consummate swimmers. Their seemingly effortless movement through water is made possible by their streamlined bodies, webbed hind feet, and unique paddlelike tails.

and branches that contains the family's living quarters. Immediate access to the internal chamber is through a submerged tunnel, which turns the lodge into a sanctuary by keeping it safe from all but the largest or most determined of predators, namely bears and man. During the winter months, in particular, when the entire structure of the lodge becomes frozen solid, it becomes effectively impenetrable.

The integrity of the lodge as a moat-bound fortress depends to a large degree on the beavers' dambuilding skills. Downstream of the lodge, branches, tree trunks, and stones are piled across the flow, cemented together with mud and plant debris. Over the years the

Beavers have helped shape the landscape, especially in the northern latitudes of North America. This massive dam built of logs, twigs, and mud has created a pond where before there was none.

dam builds up, causing the water level behind it to rise, inundating the surrounding land and further isolating the lodge. Raising the water level has the added benefit of enabling the beaver to gain swimming access to larger areas of land and to transport sizable tree trunks back to its base where they are cached, along with other plant material, in a submerged food store near the lodge. During the winter months when the surface of the water is frozen, the beavers can gain underwater access to their refrigerated larder.

Thanks to their damming activities, beavers have a profound impact on the surrounding environment which is perhaps most striking across the tundra and northern forest regions of North America. The mosaic of pools and lakes that they create greatly increases the available areas of open water and marginal vegetation. This in turn benefits the vast numbers of wildfowl and waders that are breeding visitors to these habitats during the summer months.

Having spent a long winter in its frozen, ice-bound lodge, this beaver has ventured out as the spring thaw sets in. Just like any other responsible homeowner, it inspects for damage caused by the ravages of winter and sets about repairing gaps in the dam with characteristic enthusiasm.

Having felled this aspen tree, the beaver cuts it into manageable lengths. By doing so, it ensures that all parts of the tree can be transported back to its lodge and added to the winter food supply.

By creating a flooded terrain, beavers are able to transport branches of far greater sizes than would otherwise be manageable on land. Without this advantage, it is doubtful if they could gather sufficient food reserves to last through the winter.

Rats

No discussion of rodents would be complete without a review of man's associations, past and present, with rats. Authorities recognize a considerable number of rat species around the world, and many of those from tropical countries never come in contact or conflict with human populations. However, two species, namely the brown rat and the black rat, more than make up for this shortfall and have followed man across the globe from their original ranges in Asia Minor and India respectively. Generally speaking, the brown rat is the more widespread and abundant of the two, hence its alternative name of common rat, and is the species most typically associated with farming and sewers. By contrast, the black rat's alternative name of roof rat reflects its predilection for drier sites. It is primarily a tropical species, and where it does occur in temperate zones, it is invariably associated with the ports and docks of urban areas.

Rats cause problems for man in a number of ways. Given the chance, they eat vast quantities of foodstuffs such as stored grain and vegetables, and they contaminate even more with their feces and urine. They carry contagious diseases that are spread either directly or through the actions of disease carriers such as fleas. Lastly, they cause structural damage, either by gnawing building materials or by their burrowing activities, which undermine and erode the ground, causing the collapse of buildings and roads.

If it is possible to take a dispassionate view of rats, and in particular the brown rat, they appear as truly remarkable animals. They are cunning, ingenious, and quick to take advantage of new sources of food and new ways of exploiting them. That they are intelligent, at least as far as rodents are concerned, is not in doubt, and they have a reproductive capability that more than matches their mental and physical agility. A female brown rat, for

Black rats, or roof rats, as they are sometimes known, are essentially animals of warm, tropical climates. Thanks to man, however, the species has spread beyond its natural range. With its occupation of houses and other buildings, this industrious species has avoided the rigors of more temperate climates.

Despite their common English name, brown rats are occasionally seen as darker color forms in the wild. This inherent variation is exploited by breeders of domesticated rats in order to create new and excitingly marked breeds for the pet trade.

example, can breed when she is only eight weeks old. Following a gestation period that lasts a mere three weeks, she gives birth to a litter of up to ten young and is capable of producing twelve litters a year.

It is obviously difficult to put precise figures on the economic damage caused by rats, but it certainly runs into billions of dollars worth of destruction each year to food products alone. Often more immediately apparent is the suffering caused by diseases that rats transmit, including a potentially fatal illness known as Weil's disease and *Salmonella* food poisoning. However, one disease stands alone in its strong association with rats: the bubonic plague, a wretched affliction that killed millions of people across Asia and Europe as it swept through the region intermittently from the fourteenth to the seventeenth centuries. This so-called black death persists to this day in parts of Africa and Asia. The plague bacillus is borne in the blood of rats and transmitted to humans

by the bites of rat fleas. Occasionally, rather bald statements are made about the human misery caused by rats. There is one claim that rat-borne diseases have killed more people throughout human history than have all wars combined. A difficult analysis to confirm or deny, but even if remotely accurate, it is as much a sad indictment of human behavior, as it is of the misery caused by rats.

For many people there is another, altogether more lovable, side to these animals. They are popular pets, adored by their owners for their inquisitive and seemingly affectionate natures, as well as for their cleanliness and docility. This is a far cry from the pariah status achieved by rats living wild in the modern world, and the two extremes are something of a paradox.

This eastern woodrat displays a fine array of sensory detectors in the form of long whiskers, a large nose, showy ears, and beady eyes. It needs all of these to find its food and to detect the presence of potential predators. As a group, woodrats are known for their habit of collecting sticks and twigs and piling them in mounds, which they use as dens.

As its name suggests, this eastern swamp rat from eastern Australia and Tasmania favors damp habitats such as rain forests and swamps. Not needing to drink water, it obtains sufficient moisture from its diet of fresh plant material. Unlike the majority of native Australian mammals, the swamp rat is a placental mammal and not a marsupial.

This bannertail kangaroo rat, in the American southwestern state of Arizona, is foraging for seeds and nuts on the desert floor. Large cheek pouches enable these essentially nocturnal rodents to gather and store more food than they need at any one time before returning to the comparative safety of their burrows.

VARIED CREATURES

Despite the fact that rodents vary enormously in size, most people can recognize a member of this varied group when they see one. A compact and rather squat body is generally typical, and most species have a coat of hair that is often rather coarse and loosely packed. Almost all rodents possess a relatively long and visible tail, although the shape varies tremendously across the group as a whole.

The rodent's skeleton is fairly typical of that of mammals in general. A backbone runs the entire length of the body from the base of the skull to the tip of the tail, and along its length are attached paired forelimbs, ribs, and hind limbs. The skull appears superficially similar to other mammal skulls, but a closer look at the teeth shows marked differences.

Teeth and Feeding

The most conspicuous features of the rodent skull are the paired and opposing incisors in the upper and lower jaws which are relatively long, curved, and razor-sharp at their tips. Rodents lack canine teeth, and in many species the premolars are also absent. As a result, a large gap, known as the *diastema*, is seen on both upper and lower jaws between the front incisor teeth and the molars (and sometimes premolars too) at the back of the mouth.

When it comes to feeding, a rodent's teeth are its most vital tools. All species feed by using a gnawing action in which the cutting power of the incisors is employed to good effect upon all manner of hard organic materials, such as nutshells and bark, that encase nutritious food. Clearly, the possession of canines would confer no obvious advantage to feeding in this way. The space between the front and back teeth provides a gap into which the flexible lips can close, sealing off

The beaver's front feet have long, sharp claws that help the animal manipulate and align food and building materials such as tree trunks. Used primarily for feeding, they are of little use when the beaver swims.

The autumn's bountiful supply of nuts and seeds is a godsend to most rodents, including this eastern chipmunk. With its sharp incisor teeth, objects the size of acorns can be tackled, although the chipmunk is usually sensible enough to carry its prize to a safe retreat before attempting to open the shell.

When danger threatens, many rodents, even rather dumpy species such as this hoary marmot, are capable of remarkable bursts of speed. This alert individual has just spotted the silhouette of a golden eagle in the skies above, the species' most significant predator

cult, but in extreme cases, the teeth grow along a natural curvature and eventually pierce the skull.

Although many rodents eat small animals such as insects and spiders during at least part of their lives, the diet of most consists mainly of plant material. Therefore, the animal's dentition—the arrangement and character of the teeth—is all important. When the preferred food source is encased with a hard shell or husk, gnawing and chewing ability obviously plays a key role in allowing the animal access to that food. Even with easily obtained edibles such as soft shoots, rodents (like all mammals) are still faced with the major problem that cellulose, the fundamental building material for plant cell walls, cannot be digested by the unaided mammalian digestive system. In common with many other herbivores, rodents have struck up a partnership with bacteria living within their bodies that are capable of breaking down cellulose.

There is still one final problem to be overcome, because in a rodent's digestive system, these symbiotic bacteria live in the lower part of the gut, whereas absorption of the useful nutrients they liberate can take place only higher up the intestinal tract. Since the movement of food through the gut is essentially a one-way affair, rodents overcome the problem by engaging in refection: They eat their own droppings (those that result from the first pass through the digestive system) and digest the contents once again to produce, as a consequence, a second type of feces from which almost all nutritional value and water has been absorbed.

Movement and Senses

Walking is the main means of locomotion for most rodents, so the feet generally conform to a fairly uniform design. These animals walk on their palms or soles with all five digits splayed out in an array. There is variation, however,

the mouth from debris while the animal gnaws. Once the hard job of gnawing a nutshell or tree bark is complete, feeding proper begins, and the cheek teeth (molars and in some species premolars too) are used to grind up the fibrous components of the plant material.

Rodent incisors have a hard casing of enamel only on the front edge that allows the razor-like leading edge to develop through opposing wear. Although, the incisors grow constantly throughout the rodent's life, everyday wear and tear caused by the teeth grinding against one another usually checks their length. However, should an animal become sick or the teeth misaligned in some way, then the teeth continue to grow, sometimes with fatal consequences; not only does feeding become diffi-

Sound is an important means of communication for many rodents. This arctic ground squirrel is raising the alarm with a high-pitched squeak that alerts its nearby neighbors to danger. Its wide-open mouth reveals the incisor teeth that are such a hallmark of rodents as a group.

A fallen set of antlers at first seems an unlikely subject for the gnawing attentions of this porcupine. However, attacking such hard surfaces can help keep the continual growth of the incisor teeth in check, and as an added bonus, the rodent may ingest needed supplies of calcium.

among species that live unconventional lives by rodent standards. Thus beavers, for example, have webbed hind feet to assist with swimming, while high-speed runners touch the ground with just their fingers and toes. Tails, too, vary according to function. The basic rodent tail-form is fairly long, of uniform diameter, and often essentially hairless. Beavers, however, have flattened, rudderlike tails for swimming, while the harvest mouse has a prehensile tail that is used as a fifth limb when climbing among tangled vegetation.

Wherever they occur, rodents remain ever alert to the threat of danger. This is necessary because they are hunted by a wide range of predators, ranging in size from spiders and snakes to birds and fellow mammals. Since most rodents lack any effective means of defending themselves against an attacker in a one-to-one confrontation, many find that the best defenses are an awareness of danger and an ability to escape to safety. Not surprisingly, therefore, rodents in general have highly tuned senses and are extremely responsive to sounds, vibrations, and smells; their powers of learning and association help make best use of the sensory information they receive. In addition, most seldom stray too far from potential sanctuary even in the best of times. Retreats vary from species to species, but a typical refuge might be a burrow bolt-hole for mice, voles, and rats; a tree hole for squirrels; or open water for beavers. Despite their best endeavors, countless millions of rodents are consumed each year by predators all over the world. This is part of nature's plan, for without the checks and balances of predation, the world could become overrun by those species with particularly dramatic rates of reproduction.

Rodent Classification
Biologists organize the living world into a hierarchy, grouping plants and animals according to characteristics that are either shared with one another or unique. The

Spring is a time of plenty for rodents such as woodchucks, whose diet consists mainly of the succulent new shoots and leaves of plants. The species hibernates during the winter, thus overcoming any need to alter its diet to suit seasonal changes in food availability.

smallest division is called the *species*, a group of animals capable of breeding with each other; the species is the building block of classification. At the other extreme, the broadest division within the animal kingdom is called a *phylum* and it is into one of these phyla that all vertebrates—animals with backbones—are placed. The vertebrates themselves comprise a number of further subdivisions called *classes* and one of these embraces all known mammals; other separate classes hold the fishes, amphibians, reptiles, and birds. Within the mammals class are a number of *orders*, which are further split into *suborders*, each of which contains a number of smaller divisions called *families*. The order Rodentia, in which rodents are placed, contains some seventeen hundred species, nearly forty percent of all known mammals. It is generally divided into three suborders, based on the way in which the jaw muscles are organized; by and large, these three main groupings are fairly obvious even to the casual observer.

Beavers' tails are used both for swimming and to signal danger. The animals often cruise along at the surface, but if disturbed, they submerge in an instant, slapping the water's surface with their tails. The sound of this action causes alarm among nearby members of the group.

Nocturnal habits and burrow refuges enable rodents to evade many predators, but they are of little value in avoiding snakes. Species such as this tiger rattlesnake use venom to kill their prey, while others use constriction. The end result is the same, however, and snakes are significant the world over in controlling wild populations of rodents.

Squirrel-like Rodents

Squirrel-like rodents are considered to be the most primitive of their kind. The group includes more than 370 species, classified into seven separate families: beavers, the mountain beaver, squirrels, pocket gophers, pocket mice, scaly-tailed squirrels, and the springhare. Squirrel-like rodents possess premolar teeth— one or two per jaw depending on the species—and muscles that pull the jaw forward to enable gnawing. The diet of the group consists mainly of nuts and seeds, although

flowers, shoots, and buds are consumed in spring and summer; storing of food is observed in many species.

Beavers comprise two species, the familiar North American one and its European cousin. Not to be confused with true beavers is the mountain beaver, or sewellel, a comparatively little-known rodent of the North American Pacific Northwest. The mountain beaver favors well-vegetated areas of conifer forests and spends the daylight hours underground in semicommunal burrow complexes. Only after

Few things in nature are cuter than the sight of a squirrel peering inquisitively at a human intruder into its territory. This eastern fox squirrel, though curious, is taking no chances, as it sits on the rim of a tree-hole retreat.

From a lofty look out in the trees, this Abert's squirrel watches the progress of intruders through its territory. It is not difficult to appreciate why the species gained its alternative name: tassel-eared squirrel.

The American red squirrel is a specialist cone-feeder, as shown by the gnawed and tattered remains that litter the ground in its favorite feeding areas. By dexterous use of its hands, the squirrel holds and turns the cone so the incisor teeth are employed to good advantage.

Adorned with prominent ear tufts, a kaibab squirrel forages on the ground for fallen nuts and seeds. Squirrels are observant and inquisitive animals, quick to locate and exploit any new sources of food. Some authorities consider that this race of Abert's squirrel merits separate species status.

Peering out of its daytime retreat in a tree hole, this southern flying squirrel surveys its forest domain as dusk falls. Only when it is completely dark will this charming little rodent emerge and glide from tree to tree in search of good feeding.

dark does it emerge to feed and gather plant material for underground storage.

With more than 260 species, the squirrel family is predictably a diverse one. Squirrels themselves are generally arboreal, with strong grips and large eyes, all assisting their tree-dwelling lifestyle. A large, bushy tail is also characteristic as is a coat of dense, smooth fur. This family has representatives in North America, Europe, Africa, and Asia. All squirrels are skilled leapers, but their most determinedly arboreal relatives, the flying squirrels, have gone one stage further, by evolving membranes to assist in gliding. At the other extreme, there are entirely ground-dwelling members of the group, including marmots, susliks, and prairie dogs.

Pocket gophers are unusual rodents, the thirty or so species restricted to North and Central America. Although they may appear superficially volelike, they show a number of unique characteristics. Among these are the pocketlike cheek pouches in which food is stored and which give the animals their common name. They have proportionately large front feet, used to good effect for digging, and large

heads with incisors that project beyond the closed mouth. Except during the breeding season, pocket gophers live a rather solitary life in a network of underground burrows. In prime sites, however, territories often abut one another and loose associations of animals cover large areas. Pocket gophers feed on roots, tubers, shoots, and leaves, collecting food both at and below ground level.

Pocket mice are a diverse group of rodents from North and Central America, all of which share the ability to store food in cheek pouches. All are seed-eaters and some, notably the true pocket mice, kangaroo rats, and kangaroo mice, live in the region's deserts, among the most extreme habitats for any small mammal.

Scaly-tailed squirrels are a little-known group comprising seven species, all of which live in the rain forests of equatorial West Africa. They are essentially nocturnal, arboreal animals, remarkable for their ability to glide from tree to tree after dark, aided by a membrane of skin between the front and hind legs and between the hind legs and tail.

The springhare is the sole representative of its family and is a bizarre little animal. The size of a rabbit, it looks and behaves like a cross between a squirrel and a kangaroo, having a long, bushy tail and powerful back legs that are used for leaping. Springhares are found only on the grassy plains of sub-Saharan Africa and spend much of the day within the comparative safety of their burrows. After dark they emerge to graze the surrounding vegetation. Keen senses of smell, hearing, and sight are needed to avoid the species' numerous predators, which include man.

With its large hind legs and long tail, this Ord's kangaroo rat is indeed a kangaroo in miniature. Like its marsupial namesake, this engaging little desert rodent moves by hopping, and covers a considerable range in its nightly feeding forays.

Black-tailed prairie dogs live in large communities known as "towns," within which smaller, well-defined aggregations of individuals are found. While most members of the group are feeding or resting, at least one remains on guard. When danger is spotted, this sentry raises the alarm by uttering shrill, disyllabic barking calls.

A young hoary marmot engages in one of the species' favorite pastimes, surveying the landscape from a prominent rock. The youngster will also need to spend a considerable amount of time feeding during the summer to build up enough fat reserves to sustain it through its winter hibernation.

Mouselike Rodents

In terms of sheer numbers of species and the impact that some of them have on our lives, the suborder of mouselike rodents is highly important. It includes more than 1,135 species, roughly twenty-five percent of all known mammal species. In terms of their dentition, mouselike rodents have in common with other rodents the large, paired incisors so characteristic of the group. Canine teeth are missing, of course, but so are the premolars; consequently most mice, rats, and their relatives have only three cheek teeth, or molars, on each side of each jaw. All the muscles linking the skull with the lower jaws are arranged so that they pull both upward and forward as the mouth is closed; this enhances both gnawing and grinding teeth actions in the group. The suborder Myomorpha is divided into five families, mice and rats, the dormice, the desert dormice, the jumping mice and relatives, and the jerboas.

Mice and rats comprise more than one thousand species, making the family to which they belong by far the most important rodent group. For ease of description and to better enable a grasp of relationships within the group, the family is further split into fifteen subfamilies.

Arguably, the best known members of the mice and rat family are the Old World rats and mice, such as the wood mouse, the house mouse, the black rat, and the brown rat.

All members have the same basic anatomical design. The body is sleek, slender, and covered in short hair; the ears and eyes are well developed; and the tail is proportionately long and naked. In the wild, the diet consists mainly of grain, seeds, and nuts, but members of this opportunistic group frequently take advantage of unexpected food sources.

Although a few notable species of Old World rats and mice have spread far and wide in the wake of man, a separate group of similar

Seemingly immune to the spines among which it is moving, this cactus mouse from southern desert areas of North America gains a degree of protection from predators while foraging on the plant for seeds. The animal is opportunistic and will also take insects if the chance arises.

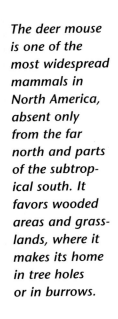

The deer mouse is one of the most widespread mammals in North America, absent only from the far north and parts of the subtropical south. It favors wooded areas and grasslands, where it makes its home in tree holes or in burrows.

Lemmings are an exclusively northern group of rodents, best known for the wild fluctuations observed in their numbers and for the "migrations" undertaken by certain species. This brown lemming is widespread on the tundra of northwest Canada and Alaska.

Mitchell's hopping mouse has perfected a burrowing lifestyle in the sandy soils of Australia. It even finds much of its food—plant shoots and roots— while digging. As its name suggests, this little rodent moves about above ground by hopping.

After the seasonal harvest of maize, fallen sweet-corn cobs provide a feeding bonanza for many rodents, including this meadow vole. As well as occurring in farmland across central and northern North America, the species also occurs in natural grassy habitats such as meadows and swamps.

rodents has evolved in the Americas. Species of the so-called New World rats and mice subfamily range throughout the northern and southern continents, and in appearance at least, many are essentially the counterparts of their Old World relatives in Europe, Asia, and Africa. For example, many deer mouse species look just like the European wood mice and fill similar niches. At the other extreme, many New World rats and mice have developed specialized habits and lifestyles. Some have a diet of insects and fish while others, notably the wood rats, create elaborate nest mounds made of twigs.

Voles and lemmings are found across northern latitudes of the Northern Hemisphere, some species penetrating deep into the Arctic. All have rather rotund and compact bodies and proportionately short tails, and all are herbivores. Most species spend the greater part of their lives in a network of burrows sited among, or just below, the surface layer of vegetation. In these retreats, they find a degree of safety from predators and insulation from the extremes of the winter climate.

Several species of gerbils are found across arid and semi-desert regions of Africa and Asia, and the bulk of the water they consume comes directly from their diet of seeds or from moisture condensed on the surface of the food itself. Although they belong to a separate subfamily, hamsters share an environment similar to gerbils across the Asiatic range. They are essentially nocturnal and store food in times of plenty in underground chambers. Other subfamily groupings within the mice and rat family include blind mole-rats, African pouched rats, African swamp rats, the crested rat, African climbing mice, bamboo rats, Madagascan rats, oriental dormice, and Asiatic mole-rats.

Following page: Confident in the certain knowledge that its spiny coat makes it invulnerable to attack, this porcupine is wandering across the forest floor. When it finds a suitable tree for feeding, the animal will make its way up the trunk, its grip aided by its long claws.

In autumn, the common dormouse of Europe feasts on the rich supply of nuts and berries found in its woodland habitat. Having put on a considerable amount of weight in the form of fat reserves, the dormouse hibernates through the winter months from October until the following April.

The eleven dormouse species are confined to Europe, western Asia, or southern Africa, and most are agile tree-climbers. European species, including the familiar and well-loved common dormouse, hibernate during the winter months. Jumping mice, as their name suggests, are good at leaping, using their enlarged hind legs and long tails for balance. Most species are essentially surface-dwellers, and some supplement a diet of seeds and grasses with invertebrates such as insects. Their close relatives, the birchmice, are nocturnal rodents that run rather than leap and spend at least part of their lives in underground burrows. They hibernate and are famed for their ability to feast or fast, depending on prevailing food supplies.

Jerboas are desert-dwelling rodents from Asia and North Africa. They dig extensive burrows using their front feet and incisors and are well-known as jumpers, having long hind legs and long tails which help counterbalance their springing movements.

Being small and generally rather secretive, native Australian rodents, such as this long-tailed mouse, receive little attention from biologists compared to larger, marsupial mammals such as kangaroos and koalas.

Using its hands to help process its food, this wood mouse from Europe is feeding unobtrusively on the woodland floor. This species is extremely important in the diet of a number of predators such as tawny owls and weasels.

Cavy-like Rodents

The body of the guinea pig is the basic anatomical plan for this suborder. There is comparatively little variation in overall proportions among the group, although considerable variation in terms of size and appearance of the coat. A cavy-like rodent has a rather plump body, a proportionately large head, a short tail, and rather slender legs; the fur varies from soft and silky in the guinea pigs themselves to spiny in the porcupines. Four cheek teeth are present on each jaw, and the skull is structured to allow the large and powerful jaw muscles to operate.

The cavies are an exclusively South American group, the most familiar member of which is the endearing guinea pig. The domesticated species is a popular pet and has lent both its name and its physiology to laboratory experiments; it is also of course relished for its meat. Several guinea pig species still occur in the wild, and other members of the family include the mara or Patagonian hare, the rock cavy, and the desert cavies.

The sole member of its group, the capybara is the largest of all rodents. At one time the species was widespread across the low wetlands of northern South America, but hunting for its pelt and meat have drastically reduced its range. Capybaras are herbivorous, amphibious, and active off and on throughout the day, although persecution by man has meant that terrestrial grazing often occurs at night.

The coypu is the solitary member of its group. Originally from southern South America, it has been farmed throughout the world for its fur, known as *nutria*, and feral populations have become established in many far-flung places. The coypu is a large, mainly aquatic rodent with a long tail. It

A capybara emerges from a South American lake to feed on waterside vegetation. This species is the largest of all rodents, and one of the most amphibious, despite lacking specific adaptations for swimming, such as webbed feet or a powerful tail.

lives in burrows in river banks and feeds largely on water plants, sometimes venturing onto neighboring dry land if the grazing is good.

Old World porcupines and New World porcupines share similarities in their appearances but are separated by their geographical ranges and their habits. The former are essentially

A prehensile tail acts as a fifth limb for this essentially arboreal tree porcupine from Central America. The spines, which cover the body of this species and other porcupines, are in fact modified hairs that serve as a deterrent to would-be attackers.

The coypu, or nutria, is one of the most amphibious of all rodents and can swim strongly, using its webbed hind feet for propulsion. Although the animal's bright orange teeth may look intimidating, their main purpose is feeding. Coypus spend most of the day resting in burrows excavated in waterside banks.

45

This agouti is found in the rain forests of Central America, where it makes a living by foraging among the leaf litter for fallen fruits. In times of plenty, agouti's bury a portion of the fruits they find; those that are not rediscovered by the rodent germinate into new trees.

Looking like a cross between a pig and a terrier, pacas are unusual rodents that live in the tropical forests of Central and South America. They are usually difficult to see, having grown wary of man as the result of being frequently hunted.

terrestrial, while the latter are at least partly arboreal, depending on the species involved. A wide range of additional cavy-like rodent families are found throughout the Americas, and these include pacas, agoutis and acouchis, chinchillas and viscachas, hutias, the pacarana, chinchilla rats, spiny rats, degus, tuco-tucos, cane rats, African rock rat, and African mole-rats.

Despite the porcupine's bizarre and unique appearance, a view of its incisor teeth leaves the observer in no doubt that the animal is indeed a rodent. Porcupines feed on the buds, twigs, and young bark of trees, including both coniferous and deciduous species.

RODENT LIFESTYLES

Rodents are adaptable and varied not only in their size and appearance, but also in their lifestyles and biology. Many have remarkable breeding rates, while others provide prolonged parental care. A few are solitary, but some lead complex social and sociable lives. These contrasts and differences make rodents a remarkable and fascinating group of animals.

Reproduction

At least part of the phenomenal success of rodents must be attributed to their powers of reproduction. In some species, the breeding rate is legendary; the numbers of young seeming to spiral out of control during times of plenty. By contrast, some rodents have comparatively modest breeding potential, which is invariably compensated for by a strategy that maximizes the survival of the next generation. Generally speaking, most rodents become sexually mature at a comparatively early age in mammalian terms, and those studied in any detail reveal that sexual behavior and physiology—notably receptivity in females—is often affected in a profound manner, or even synchronized by, chemical scents in the urine of males. Both of these adaptations contribute in no small way to rodents' reproductive success.

In the case of many rodent species, the young are born at an extremely early stage in development, well before they have any chance of fending for themselves in any way. Among the squirrels, for example, gestation may last some four to six weeks, depending on the season and the species in question. The resulting litter of five or six young is born naked and hairless. It is a further two weeks or so before fur begins to appear, another week until the teeth grow, and yet one more before the eyes open. Without the care provided by

Like others of their kind, Olympic marmots are sociable animals that live together in family groups. Play among young marmots is common, but their boisterous behavior sometimes becomes an irritation to adults that have more pressing matters of feeding and survival to contend with.

Set against the backdrop of Wyoming's Devil's Tower, this black-tailed prairie dog "town" covers a considerable area. As can be seen from the photograph, prairie dog communities have considerable local impact on their environment through their burrowing and feeding activities.

The South American tree porcupine is a skilled climber, with a powerful and confident grip. Its diet includes a wide variety of leaves, harvested from the trees, often at a considerable height above the ground.

the mother, the young of squirrels and many other related rodents have no chance whatsoever of surviving.

At the other extreme, guinea pigs, which produce litters of only three or so young, have relatively long gestation periods—fifty or so days—and produce precocious babies that are active soon after birth and have their eyes open. A similar degree of specialization is seen in New World porcupines as well, where gestation can last as long as two hundred days; one or two young are born with their eyes open and are mobile and able to climb soon after birth.

Over time all animals are affected by natural checks and balances. It is hardly surprising, therefore, when the prodigious breeding success of rodents experiences a downturn. Reproduction in desert-dwelling spiny pocket mice, for example, is linked to the flowering and seed production of desert plants. After the rains and subsequent flowering, breeding continues apace, but if the rains fail, reproduction is curtailed altogether.

Arguably, it is in the Northern Hemisphere that the most graphic evidence of rodent reproductive trends is seen with the voles and lemmings, creatures of grassland areas and tundra respectively. The populations of several species follow cyclical trends, and every three or four years reach a peak of abundance due to phenomenal reproductive success. This is followed by a crash due to catastrophic mortality. The sudden decline in numbers may be induced by starvation caused by exhaustion of food supplies, the inhibiting effects of overcrowding on reproduction, or aggression between overcrowded individuals; more likely, a range of factors is responsible.

In the Norway lemming, these cyclical trends are manifested in the legendary "migrations" undertaken by this species. Migration is perhaps the wrong word, since the mass movements of the animals are random in orientation and decidedly one-way: They are simply trying to escape from areas of overcrowding, not heading toward a desired destination. Often, vast numbers end up drowning in

In common with other mammals, rodents, such as this deer mouse, suckle their young. With most species, the babies are born at a comparatively early stage of development and are naked, blind, and helpless. The youngsters in this photograph are a mere three days old.

Thanks to the nutritious milk on which they have been feeding, these ten-day-old baby deer mice have grown considerably in weight, acquired a fur coat, and have eyes that are open to the world.

attempts to cross water. The populations of Arctic avian predators such as long-tailed skuas, rough-legged buzzards, and snowy owls are also strongly influenced by lemming cycles. In seasons when rodent numbers are high, predators do well and raise large broods. However, after a crash in lemming numbers, they may fail to breed or be absent altogether from large tracts of Arctic terrain.

Social Rodents

As any pet lover will tell you, the degree to which rodents are social animals varies, even among those few species that have been successfully domesticated. At one extreme there are hamsters, which are essentially solitary animals except for brief periods of courtship and mating. At the other are the domesticated descendants of house mice that thrive in colonies, even if these comprise groups that are sexually segregated for population control.

Solitary behavior in the wild is generally found among rodents that live in challenging, desert-like environments; hamsters and pocket gophers qualify in this respect. Some degree of contact is obviously necessary during the breeding season and is presumably inevitable to a limited extent throughout the year, except where the species in question is rare or whose precise distribution is thinly scattered. Gray squirrels are also essentially solitary animals by nature, but their arboreal territories often overlap, and animals may even congregate in places where feeding happens to be good. In common with some other rather solitary and territorial rodents such as grasshopper mice, the territory of males is larger than that of females.

Colonial behavior is also seen in a diverse range of rodents. Marmots, for example, live in groups of up to forty animals which occupy a communal network of burrows. However, perhaps the most extreme example of this

In the warmth of the evening sunlight, a herd of capybaras emerges from a wetland pool in Venezuela to graze on the marginal vegetation. This giant among rodents reaches an adult size that is much the same as a full-grown sheep.

Under the watchful eye of its mother, this young North American porcupine is practicing climbing, a skill that will stand it in good stead later in life. The species spends much of its life feeding and resting in trees.

lifestyle, in terms of numbers at least, is seen in prairie dogs. In sites where they pose no threat to man's agricultural activities and are left to their own devices, these engaging rodents form townships which can be one hundred acres or more in extent. Although at first glance these towns may appear communal, there is a distinct structure to their social organization, the whole made up of relatively small groups of animals called *coteries*, each one having its own defined territory within the burrow system as a whole.

Partly on account of their large size, it is difficult to miss the fact that capybaras are social animals. For much of the year, these giants of the rodent world live in groups comprising ten to twenty animals, although during the dry season, several groups may come together,

The social fabric of black-tailed prairie dog life is important to the integrity of their communities, and bonding and greeting ceremonies are common. On occasion, neighboring individuals may even share items of food in the name of mutual harmony.

concentrated around the few remaining water holes. A typical group might include a dominant male, five or six mature females, and a number of young animals and subordinate males. Females give birth to well-developed young which are active after only a few days and soon join the group. Suckling and nursing is undertaken not only by the mother but by any other lactating female in the group.

An even more complex and structured social life is found in a relative of the capybara, the Patagonian mara. These extraordinary rodents, which look as if they are the result of a cross between a rabbit and an antelope, appear to pair for life. Even outside the breeding season, pairs remain together, although they generally shun the company of others of their kind. During the breeding season, however, a transformation takes place with up to a dozen or more pairs coming together at a communal den, where the young, generally three per female, are born and lodged. They remain at these *creches* for the next few months, visited on a regular basis by the adults and fed by the appropriate biological mothers.

Following page: For northern temperate rodents such as this eastern chipmunk from northeast North America, hibernation during the winter months is common. For most of this period, the animal's body temperature drops to a few degrees above freezing and its metabolic rate slows down.

Unusual Adaptations

Most rodents are well known for their resourceful behavior, especially when it comes to taking opportunistic advantage of food supplies. Being adaptable and intelligent is an obvious advantage for any animal. But for species that live in often challenging environments, physical and physiological adaptations, evolved through generations of natural selection, are equally important.

In many parts of the global range of rodents, food supplies are seasonal or unpredictable, thus placing a strain on the survival of all animals. Desert-dwelling rodents are often dependent on the annual rains to induce blossoming and, hence, seed production in the hardy flowers of this arid habitat. Breeding is often timed to coincide with seed production and may even be abandoned during periods of prolonged drought, causing population numbers to decline markedly. It might be supposed that the supply of water itself would be a limiting factor, but gerbils, for example, get all the fluid they need from their diet of dry seeds. These are harvested after dark when moisture has condensed on the husk surfaces. This small amount of water is efficiently maximized by the gerbil's digestive system, and the animal is sustained.

Another approach to variable food supply is to store it in times of plenty. Some desert species adopt this method, but it is observed more readily among gray squirrels. In this species, the autumn harvest of seeds and nuts is not only an immediate source of food, but excess is cached in underground larders for use during the winter months when feeding is difficult.

An alternative approach to survival during times of hardship is hibernation, an adaptation clearly used to full advantage by the common dormouse of Europe. This endearing

Pocket mice are so called because of their fur-lined cheek pouches in which food is stored. Several species occur in western North America, and all are essentially nocturnal animals of arid terrain that spend their days in underground burrows. This desert pocket mouse is found mainly in the southwestern United States.

species is sometimes known as the hazel dormouse because of the importance of the autumn supply of hazelnuts in its pre-hibernation diet. From October to April, it enters a state of torpor, usually in an underground nest of woven surroundings, and the heart and breathing rates also slow down. Despite the almost complete shut-down in metabolic processes, the dormouse still loses up to half its body weight during hibernation, this is clearly a risky process. Though it might appear that hibernation is a method of avoiding the cold winter temperatures, it is worth noting that many other small mammals remain active in the same habitat. The dormouse's torpor probably has more to do with the almost complete absence of food available to an exclusively arboreal mammal during the winter. After its awakening in spring, the dormouse feeds on flowers and insects to build up its reserves, but it still does not abandon its sleepy lifestyle. It is essentially nocturnal in its feeding habits, entering a state known as summer torpor during the day.

With rather squat bodies and proportionately short legs, most rodents scamper, run, or walk as they make their ways around their particular environments. For some species, however, these rather mundane methods of movement have been supplemented or even abandoned in favor of more exotic ways of moving about.

As a group, ground squirrels are widespread down the western half of North America, with a range of different species occupying habitats as varied as arctic tundra, mountain grasslands, and prairies. Some species have even evolved to live in deserts, where they forage among the cacti.

Common dormice are among the sleepiest of all mammals. Not only do they hibernate during the winter months—from October to April—but in the summer they enter a state of torpor during the daytime, becoming active only after dark.

In most years, arctic ground squirrels hibernate from October to May in underground burrows, where they keep a store of food—nuts and seeds mainly—as a provision for the spring. From time to time during the winter, however, animals occasionally wake up and investigate the outside world briefly before returning to sleep.

Unlikely Habits

At first glance, an aquatic lifestyle might seem an unlikely one for a rodent, but nevertheless, several species have taken to the freshwater environment and thrived. The European water vole, for example, is able to swim with ease both on the surface and submerged, despite the fact that it does not show any conspicuous adaptations to this means of locomotion. Coypus on the other hand have webbed feet and a thick outer layer of coarse fur overlying a dense, water-resistant underfur. With the possible exception of the beaver, they are perhaps the most amphibious of all rodents.

Several rodent species from arid, open terrain, such as kangaroo rats and the springhare, have taken to hopping around their environment in the manner of miniature kangaroos;

the superficial similarities between these two unrelated groups of animals is reinforced by their long legs and long tail. Speed of movement is obviously greatly enhanced by the ability to hop, and as a consequence, these species can forage over far larger areas than can their cousins whose movement is achieved more conventionally. Being able to hop quickly presumably improves the chances of escaping from predators, but this advantage is probably offset by the fact that as the distance a rodent roams from the sanctuary of its burrow increases, the chances of reaching safety in an emergency diminish.

It is hardly surprising that arboreal mammals such as squirrels have acquired a confidence off the ground that enables them to climb with ease and to leap from branch to branch,

The European water vole is the most aquatic member of its family and can swim and dive with ease. In sites where they are not disturbed, these charming rodents will sit and feed at regular spots on the bank, seemingly indifferent to the gaze of observers.

seemingly without a moment's hesitation. Some species make more use of their jumping abilities than others and exercise a degree of influence over distance and direction by splaying their legs and generally flattening the body to increase the body surface area. A number of specialist forest species have taken the process one stage further and have evolved a means of transforming their leaps into precision glides. These are the so-called flying squirrels, a diverse group of rodents from a number of genera.

Seen running up the trunk of a tree or negotiating a gnarled or twisted branch, flying squirrels can look rather cumbersome, the flaps of skin along their sides seemingly impairing their ability to move with the freedom of other arboreal rodents. Once one of these amazing animals launches itself into mid-air, however, all thoughts of awkwardness are immediately dispelled as the animal glides effortlessly from one tree to another. In some species, distances of more than 250 feet (75 meters) may be covered; the duration of the glide enabling the observer to get a good look at the structure of the animal. With its legs spread-eagled, membranes of skin between the front and hind legs can be seen clearly. Minor adjustments to the speed and angle of flight are achieved by stretching or relaxing the

membrane tensions on either side of the body and by flexing the tail. The ability to glide from one tree to another allows flying squirrels to explore and exploit new feeding grounds with ease. It also enables them to escape from arboreal mammalian predators. The fact that many flying squirrel species are often nocturnal may reflect the fact that, despite their skills in the air, they are still vulnerable to diurnal birds of prey.

The little saltmarsh harvest mouse has an extremely restricted distribution and is found only around San Francisco Bay. As its name suggests, it favors areas of saltmarsh—an unusual habitat for a rodent—and appropriates the abandoned nests of song sparrows, customizing them to its own needs.

Coypus make their dens in burrows excavated in the banks of rivers and wetlands, where they occur. Not surprisingly, this activity leads eventually to erosion of the dry land, and the presence of these sizable rodents is generally less than welcome in farming areas.

Caught in midair, this southern flying squirrel clearly shows the membranes that stretch between the front and hind legs, enabling it to glide with consummate ease. Direction is controlled by use of the tail and through subtle differential flexing of the membranes on the right and left side of the animal.

White-footed mice are among the most agile of rodents. Not only can they run and climb with speed and confidence, but also they can leap from branch to branch covering distances of several feet in a single bound.

Among North American rodents, the southern flying squirrel is the most skilled aeronaut. This delightful little animal is strictly nocturnal, but despite being hampered by lack of light, it is able to glide from tree to tree with great confidence.

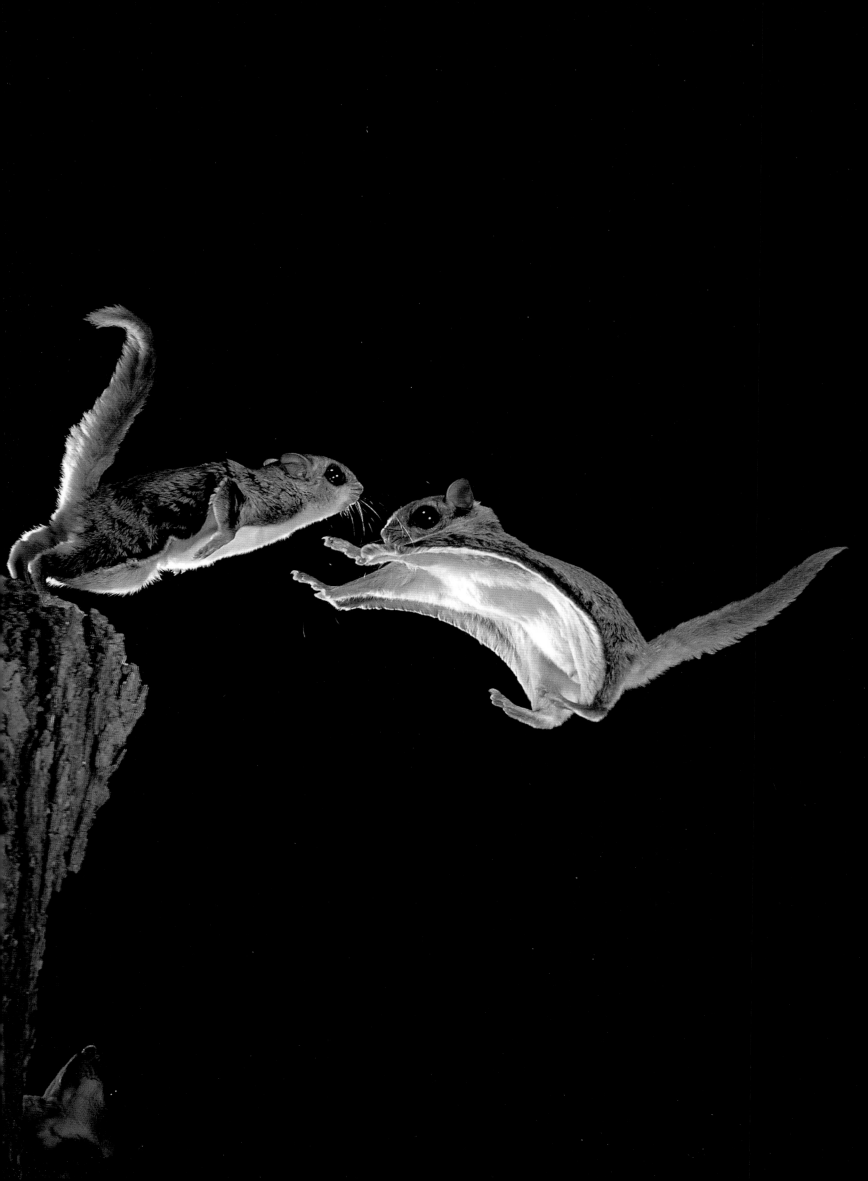

Rodents and Man

Man has had associations with his rodent neighbors throughout recorded history, and directly or indirectly, this varied group of animals has had a greater influence on the numbers, health, and demography of human populations than any other mammals. A few species fulfill positive roles, but others are almost totally negative.

Of the seventeen hundred or so rodent species currently known, only a handful are responsible for the often extraordinary impact the group has on human lives.

Food, Fur, and Pets

Since many rodent species achieve a reasonable size and some are abundant, it is surprising how few are actually considered worth eating. In South America, the most important edible species is the guinea pig, which lends itself to domestication and is featured on the menus of households and restaurants to this day, especially in countries down the Andean spine of the continent. The largest of all rodents, the capybara, is also eaten, and since a full grown adult is the size of a sheep, it can provide a considerable amount of meat. The species is farmed, or at least managed in some way in Venezuela, but elsewhere in South America, it has been hunted more indiscriminately and has consequently disappeared from much of its former range. Capybaras are also important for their pelts, as are coypus and, of course, beavers. Guinea pigs and hamsters are among the most valued pets, and it is perhaps ironic that rats and mice—the rodent species that causes the greatest economic damage—are also highly prized companions too.

Pests

As we have seen, some rodent populations remain stable year after year, while breeding results in other species are cyclical, resulting in occasional periods when the animals are super-abundant. On these occasions certain species come into conflict with human economic activities. For example, certain species of meadow voles can have a devastating effect upon forest plantations by gnawing young saplings. Commercial damage to trees is not limited to voles, however, and gray squirrels, whose numbers essentially remain stable, can play havoc in a woodland by their bark-stripping feeding habits.

Following page: Stored grain and cereals act as magnets for many rodent species, such as these white-footed mice. Their prodigious appetites, and the fact that they spoil more than they eat, lead many rodents into conflict with man.

The original, natural distribution of the European house mouse is almost impossible to assess, since the species has spread far and wide in the wake of man. As its name suggests, it often occupies human dwellings, although it is more usually associated with barns and outbuildings where foodstuffs are stored

You need to take to the air to appreciate fully the impact that beavers have on the northern landscape. Were it not for the damming activities of these industrious animals, the ponds that dot the landscape would not exist.

The Old World harvest mouse, one of the smallest rodents, occurs from western Europe to the Asian shores of the Pacific. It prefers to live in areas of tall vegetation, but will inhabit structures such as barns and storage facilities. Up to five thousand animals have been found in buildings of this kind.

In the wilderness, humans can only admire the industry and careful planning of beavers. However, in parts of North America where commercial land interests prevail, the activities of these imposing rodents are often less than welcome. The damming of watercourses and the resulting inundations have a potentially catastrophic effect on areas of forestry and farming, as well as a destructive impact on trees caused by feeding.

Mice and several species of rats cause considerable damage to growing crops and, of course, can have a devastating impact on stored food products such as grain, vegetables, and fruit. Their populations are seldom cyclical in the way that those of voles are. That rodents compete with us for the food we grow should come as no surprise. The large scale of farming seen today creates a limitless resource for our competitors, and their numbers simply reflect the results of human endeavors.

Apart from the brown rat, the house mouse is arguably our most familiar rodent companion, and it has probably been with us since the days our early ancestors first started to cultivate cereals. It has followed in the wake of man and his agriculture around the world and, as its English name suggests, is no stranger to urban life. Indeed, house mice are a familiar sight to this day in the underground transport networks of London, New York, and many other major cities. Here they arouse mild curiosity, but when they invade food stores, eating and contaminating grain or pulses for example, the response they receive is understandably more hostile.

For as long as rodents have lived alongside humans, control of their numbers has been a problem. Eradication has generally proved to be an impossible task, and the use of poisons and predators reduces their populations only temporarily. Love them or loathe them, rodents are here to stay and will continue to plague and fascinate humans as they have throughout history.

The beaver's efficiency and amazing ability to fell tall trees is viewed as a threat when it invades areas devoted to timber growing and farming.

INDEX

*Page numbers in **bold-face** type indicate photo captions.*